How to be the Perfect Husband

A short guide for males who are, or are about to become, husbands.

How to be the Perfect Husband

A short guide for males who are,
or are about to become, husbands.

by Mungo Auchinleck

How to be a Perfect Husband.

Copyright © Colin Affleck.

ISBN: 978-1-7771180-0-6

Published in Hawkesbury, March 2020.

*À ma belle Ghislaine,
la femme parfaite.*

Introduction

Starting now, I am going to assume you are a male. If you are not, stop reading, put the guide down and walk away. This is confidential man-to-man stuff.[1]

First of all, why would you want to be a perfect husband? The answer is that most basic of motives:

It's in your own best interest.

Life is short and filled with trials, tribulations and problems. Would it not be a good thing if those trials were fewer, those tribulations were shorter, those problems were less frequent? You bet it would. And as marriage, and all that it includes, eats up (or will eat up) a huge percentage of that short time allotted to you, why would you not want that period to be as pleasant, as enjoyable and as smooth as possible? Imagine being married to someone who thought you were wonderful, who describes in glowing detail to her friends how thoughtful you are, how considerate you are, how loving and supportive you are and who, as a result of your efforts, responded by trying to anticipate what you want, to cater to your needs and to become, in turn, the perfect wife. Now imagine this happy state of affairs going on for the rest of your life. This, my friend, is something close to paradise. (Unless, that is, you are into some sort of masochistic, 'I must be unhappy and suffer' thing in which case, buying this guide was a huge waste of good money.) It seems pretty logical, therefore, that as we are all almost certainly going to end up married, and we all want that married state to be

---

[1] And while I'm on the subject, it's not politically correct stuff either. If you want gender neutral, feminist friendly, socially acceptable, useless pablum, go elsewhere.

one of blissful happiness, that we all should give our present or upcoming role as husband some serious thought. Oddly, to me anyway, very few of we males actually do that.

It's true. Marriage is a stage into which most all of us will enter yet which curiously few of us will really understand or have even considered. The surprises, the disappointments, the confusion, which are certain to arise, all stem from this lack of understanding about just what the heck we have got ourselves into. The discussion which follows in this guide should help explain some elements of marriage you may not have considered and, following that, why striving to become the perfect husband makes, in the end, perfect sense.

***Note:** Throughout this guide, I use the words 'married' or 'marriage'. Sometimes I refer to a 'wife' or a husband'. I do this for simplicity's sake. Unstated but implied, this also includes all those male and female persons who live in the states of common law, co-habitation or any similar union. (See 'Why Get Married?' below.)*

Table of Contents

Training for Marriage   **1**
  What it means (and doesn't mean)
  to be a perfect husband.   1
  Why Get Married?........................2
  Laying the Foundation.........................3
  Knowing Yourself.........................3
  Choosing the Optimum Woman 8

Taking the Plunge.
That's You, Married.   **13**
  This Odd Creature, Your Wife.................. 14
  But....Attentive How?....................... 19
  Courting Behaviour 19
  Sex.................................... 36
  Cheating on your Wife...................... 36

The Perfect Husband, summarized   **41**

The Appendices   **43**
  Appendix A: Reproductive Strategies 43
  Appendix B: The Selection Process............... 45
  Appendix C: Courting Behaviour................. 46

Training for Marriage

What it means (and doesn't mean) to be a perfect husband.

So, what is a perfect husband? Every woman asked is going to give you a different answer to this question and so, to avoid confusion, we just won't ask them. Instead, the collective wisdom and experience of millions of your brothers out there has been compiled, collated, summarized and placed here in this guide for your benefit. You're welcome. Read on.

First, what it's not. Being a perfect husband is not being a hen- pecked, cringing, nervous servant, always living in fear of the next order from 'she who must be obeyed'. In fact, the perfect husband is just the opposite of this subordinate, subservient wretch. A one-sided marriage, where all the authority rests with only one half, is rarely a happy thing and, in today's divorce-easy climate, it will, in all likelihood, have only a short, and ugly, lifespan. Unless, of course, we are back to that mistress-slave thing and that's a whole different guide.

As a generalization, most women are looking for a partner, which evolution translates into looking for a male of relatively high quality who will assist her in raising a family.[2] The perfect husband, there-

---

[2] This looking for a potential father for her offspring may or may not be a conscious choice on her part. Evolution has programmed her in that way just as it has programmed you and me in another. After all, if it was just companionship she wanted, she'd be much better off with another woman who at least shared her values and interests AND left the seat down. If it was sex, she'd just visit a bar. Unlike us males, females generally have few problems getting all the sex they want. Nope, all the evidence points towards females searching out male partners solely because their programming, consciously or not, is pushing them to reproduce and that means hooking up with the opposite gender, however grubby and uncouth we may be.

fore, is one who first, appears to fully meet that need and then, goes one step beyond. Through observation, listening and analysis, he not only discovers what it is that his wife wants or thinks she wants. He will, over time and with constant attention, actually anticipate those things. The perfect husband, then, is one that through his actions and attitudes, reassures the woman that she made not only the right choice, she has won the man lottery.

Why Get Married?

Because you have few other options. Let's work it out. You want to have and hold this woman, to the exclusion of all other males, forever. Right? Fair enough. That means married. Think you're not married if there was no ceremony? Think again. True, a formal, official marriage, as in a church wedding, is on the decline in our culture. For the purposes of this guide, however, that does not matter in the least. Both the law and society are steadily making any difference between formal marriage, living common law or just co-habiting, irrelevant. If you think you can dodge the bullet, avoid the legal consequences of sharing a roof and a bed with a human female by not actually standing up in front of a minister, priest, rabbi, mullah or JP beforehand, then you, my friend, are sadly mistaken. Ask any lawyer. In spite of what your testosterone soaked brain is telling you, in this day and age if you want her all for yourself forever, you have to 'legally' marry her and today that increasingly means simply living under the same roof for a certain amount of time.[3]

---

[3] Virtually every country, province and state have, or are putting on the books, laws governing the legal responsibilities attached to each person in any of the possible 'married' variations. Living with a female now has, and will increasingly come to have, significant legal consequences. (In Ontario, for example, you could have some legal obligations after only one year, or less depending on the relationship.) Do not assume anything. You are the one who will have to face the music if it goes bad. Carefully check the appropriate level of government website in your jurisdiction for the scary details and / or have a chat with your favourite lawyer.

How to be the Perfect Husband

Laying the Foundation

Like building a house, everything about being the perfect husband needs to rest on a well-thought-out, solid foundation. In this case, that foundation is twofold: (These are important. Note them down. Perhaps tattoo them on your arm.) **Knowing Yourself** and **Choosing the Optimum Woman**[4] .

Knowing Yourself

First, knowing yourself. What does that mean? And what does that have to do with being the perfect husband? It means before making the plunge into marriage, taking a long, hard look in the mirror and being brutally honest. It means looking beyond what you wish you were, seeing past what you hope others think of you and finally stopping with all that adolescent posing and attitude nonsense. And if you think that's easy, or you can do it in the space of time you need to drink a beer with your buddies, you are already on the wrong track.

Consider that solid foundation analogy used above. In a marriage, there are, or will be, an unlimited number of unknowns, variables, shifting tides and surprises and some will come from that woman you now, or will soon, call your wife. You will be repeatedly blindsided and confused by events you just did not expect and did not see coming. How will you handle all that? Get mad? Get drunk? Run away? Those routes are for the weak

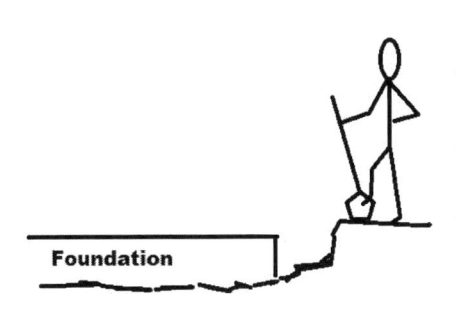

---

[4] In point of fact, it is actually the female who does the choosing, making her selection based on those males available in her time and place. However, as following that idea will simply lead us into a quagmire of evolutionary and anthropological theory, let's stick with the commonly held misbelief that it's the males who, by choosing to go down on bended knee, select their woman. For a bit more on this, please see Appendix B.

and the stupid. Besides, none of them really work. Not really in the short term and definitely not really in the long haul. There must be one solid point of reference for you when the confusion strikes: one calm, solid rock you can stand on when the storm hits, one thing that you know for certain and can totally rely on as a starting point to deal with any problem. That thing is you.

Knowing yourself can be most simply explained as having confidence in yourself. In knowing who you are, knowing your capabilities, knowing your strengths and knowing your weaknesses. It can also be called maturity. You are all grown up now; you don't have to strut and pose like an adolescent to show what a man you are. There is no need. You are what you are, and you know it. In my experience, it is the guys who feel the need to shout, threaten, pose and dominate both women and other males who are themselves the least confident. They are trying to compensate for an inner doubt about themselves, trying to drown out a nagging voice that tells them they are not all they claim to be, that they have a hidden weakness which they must desperately hide both from women and other males. To be an obnoxious, loud, trouble-making bully in high school is more or less normal. It's even thought to be pretty cool. But not for long. It is a phase males go through as they mature but those actions are not those of a man. If as an adult you still feel the need to act the same way, chances are you have a maturity or self image problem which will make your becoming the perfect husband much more difficult, if not impossible. Too bad. You lose.

So, how do you get this insight into who and what you really are? By critical thinking,

How to be the Perfect Husband

that's how. Forget your friends; forget all the blah-blah on your smart phone. Forget Google or what the self-help sites say. This one is yours alone.

Are you mature enough yet for asking and answering the tough questions? I have no idea. Only you would know that and maybe even you're not sure. Look in the mirror. Why do you act the way you do? Who are you trying to impress or intimidate? (And if you say nobody, I'll say bullshit.) And why is that so important to you? Who are you really? What do you think your good points are? What things about yourself are you ashamed of, embarrassed by or just want to keep private? (You say nothing? Again, bullshit.) Why those things? And why are those things such a big deal for you? Who are you when it's just you, by yourself, alone in the room?

It's perfectly normal for a young male to desperately want to impress the girls and the other guys. To try to project an image of strength, power and confidence. It's a competitive world out there and especially so for young males. Obsessing about your physical strength (or lack thereof), your size, your looks, your toughness and image, about what you hope others think of you, all that is just par for the course, so don't feel too badly about having been like that. But don't stay there either. As a teenager you don't have the experience to see past your raging hormones. Everything is instinct. But now that you are all grown up, what's your excuse? The reality is that no one gives a crap about you and your self image. All that matters out there in the big world is, are you a mature, adult male or are you not? Do you see yourself clearly (including all your faults and weaknesses) in the light of day or do you not? If you do, if you are being honest with yourself about who you are, you may have the making of a perfect husband. If not, go back to being a little boy.

So how will your being confident about yourself affect your

marriage or being the perfect husband? Like this. If you approach marriage with your eyes wide open, knowing exactly who you are, what your good and bad points are, with nothing to prove or 'show' or display, you are far stronger and better able to deal with the whole issue of marriage, even before it starts. For example, in spite of being seriously attracted, maybe marriage for you is a bad idea right now. You are just not ready. This realization can be both painful and embarrassing to you as well as upsetting to those around you but, because you are now being honest with yourself, and truly understand your own strengths and weaknesses, you suck it up, look the truth squarely in the eye and admit it to be so. If you are confident about your real self, you can see this truth clearly, admit it to yourself and others (including her) and move on.[5] People (maybe including her) will criticize you but that's okay. You know yourself and, if not exactly happy about it, you are satisfied with your decision. In the long run, both of you will win. Heck, later, she might even thank you.

Or perhaps you are enamoured (read crazed with lust) for the lady. So, in an effort to rationalize what is actually just a very strong sexual attraction, you try to convince her, yourself and everyone else that she is truly the woman you want to spend the rest of your life with. You are trying to fool yourself and that is not only never a good idea but one which, in the case of a marriage, is guaranteed to end badly, especially for you. Way better for everyone, especially you, if you know yourself, recognize your weakness for what it is (arguably the most common male weakness)[6] and move on.

And if you have actually made the big step into marriage (and sooner or later most all of us will) knowing yourself, being confident about who you are gives you the further confidence to be honest with yourself and your now wife. As soon as you start to hide stuff from her or yourself, to pretend, to not admit to weaknesses or failings,

---

[5] And have the guts and courtesy to tell her up front. Not after she has begun making plans for "her big day".

[6] Better see Appendix A

the rot begins. Untreated, it will grow like a cancer, destroy your marriage and quite possibly ruin the rest of your time here on planet earth. One lie leads to another. False emotions must be displayed, real emotions hidden, unhappy truths never spoken. Suspicions begin, unhappiness grows.

Knowing yourself, being confident about yourself, gives you the strength to admit to being weak. Sound like a contradiction? Not a bit. It takes a strong, confident man to admit that he, or the marriage, has a problem. It's the weakling who tries to hide it or bluff their way along, too afraid, too lacking in confidence to face reality.

Confidence, knowing yourself, also allows you to live comfortably with this other person. You do not need subservience from her, you do not need to dominate the relationship to reinforce your ego, you do not need to win all the arguments. You are a confident, adult male and you know it. You can speak your mind without shouting, applaud her abilities when they appear (and they will) and graciously accept criticism when it is justified. If you feel the burning need to show 'who wears the pants in this family' or 'who the man of the house is', then your marriage and your life are in for a rough ride. A real man, a confident, self-assured man who knows himself well, has no need for such antics. He already knows who and what he is and is comfortable with that.

I know who I am

and I've nothing left to prove.

So, to summarize, if you are considering marriage and want to maximize the experience by becoming the perfect husband, start by looking at yourself and asking, 'Who and what am I? What are my strengths and good points? What are my weaknesses and bad points? Why do I want to get married? And why to this woman?' Which segues nicely into the next section...

Choosing the Optimum Woman

Now here, I must confess to a bias. I believe women are, in a word, wonderful. They are beyond question my favourite half of our species, and not just because of that lust thing (though that is no doubt a factor.) While it is admittedly a huge generalization, and with many exceptions, women are on the whole more pleasant to look at than us, they are neater, they smell nicer, they are, relative to males, quieter, more thoughtful, less prone to unprovoked aggression and less likely to break the law. Women are more softly rounded; they don't have our sharp edges. All in all, women are nicer to be around. I also admire their ability to spring back from adversity, to remain committed and loyal to a person or an ideal, sometimes long after they should. And I marvel at their innate ability to fashion a home, a place of shelter, just about anywhere. They are also wonderfully mysterious. They have their own way of approaching things, of dealing with problems and yet remaining focused on the core issue. All in all, I must confess I am a big fan.

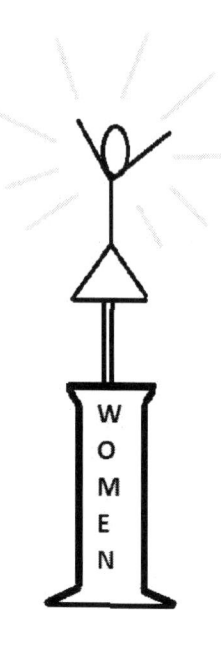

It is very difficult, perhaps impossible, to become the perfect husband if you are married to a woman who is incapable of appreciating your efforts. She will never be pleased or satisfied and you will never reap the rewards of being 'perfect'.[7] Therefore, it's clear that selecting a woman who can appreciate what she's got going here will be <u>critical</u> to your attaining perfect husband status. Below, we talk about how to choose such an op-

---

[7] If you are presently married to one of those women who does not and never will appreciate your efforts to please her, my condolences. Been there, done that. And perhaps you'll have, like me, better luck choosing next time.

How to be the Perfect Husband

timum woman. (Keeping in mind Footnote #4.)

I once read of a bitter old man saying to the young man who was contemplating marriage, "Before you ask her, lad, take a damn good look at her mother!" This is only one of many pieces of advice available out there to the prospective groom. Some is good, some bad, some indifferent. Because both you and your intended are unique individuals, there is no perfect template that you can apply to choosing a wife. What is okay for one person may be poison for another. But there are, however, general guides that will be of considerable help. To begin, ask yourself the following questions:

Can she cook? Nah, just kidding. Now for the actual questions.

Do you like her? This does not mean do you want to jump her bones every time you see her, though that's a nice thought too. No, it means do you feel at ease when she's around. Do you feel comfortable just hanging out with her? If not, why not?

Can you speak openly with her? If there are certain subjects (sex, religion, children or finances for example) that either she or you simply will not discuss, you might want to ask yourself why. [8]

Do either of you expect the other one to change to accommodate them? Some change is of course inevitable as you adapt to being a pair rather than a single, but if getting married demands a radical switch in behaviour or attitude by one of you, this will forever remain (perhaps buried deep) a fault line in the marriage. Religion, politics, gender roles and spending habits all come to mind. Do not assume. Find out where you differ and if it matters to either of you

---

[8] I digress but anecdotally, I have read that back in the Victorian era, young grooms of sufficient means often felt it necessary to obtain direction from a medical doctor so as to know exactly what was expected of them on their wedding night. This taboo subject had never been spoken of or taught to them beforehand and so, except for instinct, they arrived at their wedding night totally ignorant about sex and the female anatomy. Amazing.

enough to reconsider. Later is too late.

Are you just temporarily infatuated? There is, apparently, some evidence that falling in love produces an actual, measurable change in our body chemistry which skews our perception of our beloved somewhat. And there is a ton of hard evidence that lust will do the same. Blinded by love and/or lust, you rush in and propose, determined to have her all for yourself forever. Whoa. Take a deep breath and calm down. Marriage is not for the weekend. It's for years and years and you will be on the hook (legally) regardless of how it turns out. Step back for a moment. Try to imagine her as old, fat and grey because, someday, both she and you will be exactly that. Hold that mental picture in your mind. What do you think of her now?

Do you trust her? This can mean a number of different things beyond just her honesty when she talks with you but principally, it means is she a flirt? What she calls just 'having fun' or 'expressing herself' may later look to you awfully like flirting and nothing, literally nothing, will destroy a marriage quicker. Keep in mind that she may have the same opinion of you. Get that clarified between you ASAP and well in advance of any wedding plans.

How is she with money? Various studies have suggested that up to 80% of all marriage break-ups have their roots in money. Whether that figure is accurate or not, it is beyond doubt that those financial arrangements, or a lack thereof, are major contributing factors to marriages ending. Getting it clear beforehand where the money is coming from, where it is going to and who decides what to spend is critical. While every relationship will vary somewhat, two things are certainly going to change for you. First, you are no longer going to have complete and absolute control of your finances. Saying 'Well, I earned it so it's mine!' will simply no longer be true or acceptable. She too, and not just you, will have a say in where your money goes. And second, your free and easy days of spending what you make are over. You will have joint expenses (home, insurance, groceries, vehicle, utilities, etc) that will simply eat up what you now spend on travel, restaurants and partying. Does she understand this? Do you? Understand this now or be very disappointed later.

How do you feel about children? These may or may not be on your radar screen but, and despite what she may say out loud, they are certainly on hers whether it's immediately or at some later date. (If you are asking why, it's time to read Appendix A.) Think carefully on this. You are about to commit to marriage, a big thing. Once babies start to appear, it becomes a huge, all-encompassing thing which will affect you for the remainder of your life – whether married to her, married to someone else or not married at all. Again, think carefully on this. Ask her opinion and listen very, very closely to the answer and how it's delivered. How does that answer appear to mesh with what you think?

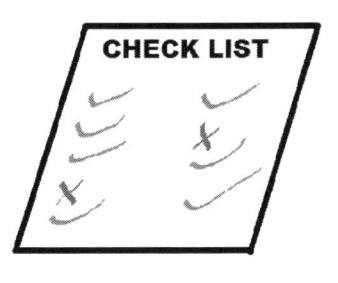

Are you ever ashamed of her or does she embarrass you in some way? Her looks, her speech, her clothes, her attitudes or opinions, her mannerisms? Do you find yourself apologizing for her? This does not necessarily mean she is wrong for you but, it is a warning. Proceed with caution. Perhaps others are seeing (and you are sensing) something you are denying to yourself. You would not be the first.

Are you overtly proud of her? Generally, this is a good thing but ask yourself this. What is it exactly I'm proud of? Is it that she is 'traffic-stopping hot' to look at? Just keep in mind it's temporary. Whether her angelic face and devilish body deteriorate slowly or quickly, you will still be married to her when it happens. Is it her achievements? Being a doctoral candidate or speaking six languages is pretty impressive, it's true, but neither one of those is going to help her husband when he feels down or support him when he needs it. Are you proud of her as person, as a partner, as a friend? Much better. That will count now AND in the long run.

While by no means all the questions you should be asking, the above are perhaps some of the more important ones you should ask yourself about your choice of woman. Now for a couple of practical tips:

Tip #1. Think you know her? Before the wedding, before the engagement, before the promises of eternal love, try the "travel together across the country in a car or van" method of evaluation Nothing five-star or luxurious, mind you. Make it all low-end economy motels or, even better, camping. The idea is for the two of you to be up close and personal under mildly stressful circumstances for a longish period of time, say two to six weeks. How did it work out? Now that you have seen her without makeup or dressed for a date, what do you think? Does she snore, talk or thrash in her sleep, insist you stay awake, or go to bed, as she does? Is she a slob? Too neat? How does she respond to a minor crisis? Maybe she's just boring, weird or narrow-minded. Or maybe she is perfect for you. (Wonder what her evaluation of you is?)

Tip #2. Do you have any close friends whose judgement you trust? If yes, and long before you go telling the world you are engaged, arrange a dinner party, a get together, whatever, where she can talk and interact with them. A night club is a bad idea here. What's needed is an opportunity for a fairly small group (a mix of males and females is best) to see her expressions and body language and listen to her thoughts. Then, later, listen to what they have to say about her. They may confirm your opinions, or they may point out something you have overlooked or are trying not to see.

Taking the Plunge. That's You, Married.

So, you've done it. That's you married. Welcome to a whole new chapter in your life. Now, how are you going to make it a great chapter, a really interesting, stimulating, positive chapter? Not sure? Don't know? Don't care? Because if that's the case, your chapter may come to resemble something from a horror story rather than a happy period in your life. Marriage is not just a curious state you happen to be in at the moment. It has now become your occupation. In fact, assuming you want to both make it work and enjoy the ride, it is now your main occupation and something that must be attended to and worked at continuously. And along the way, you just might become that person which all insightful males aspire to be, the perfect husband.

To become skilled at marriage, and so become a perfect husband, you need, like any other skill, to study it, practice it and work at it. This is not just a case of remembering her birthday. That one's so basic it can be accomplished by even the ordinary, ho-hum husband. Nor is it a case of lavishing her with expensive gifts. She'd like those, obviously, but they are not at all necessary and frankly, unless you're made of money, that's a sucker's game. You will both go broke and tire yourself out looking for better and better gifts, all to no worthwhile end. No, the perfect husband is he who, first, very carefully, considers the needs, wants and requirements of his wife and then, exceeds them.

This Odd Creature, Your Wife.

You may have noticed that females are different from us, and I don't just mean the way all their various parts move around so nicely under their clothes. They seem to have different priorities than males, a different focus, and to care more, or to care less, about different things. If you have not noticed these phenomena, *wake up*! because taking note of those differences and responding to them is fundamental to your becoming the perfect husband. Consider the next three paragraphs and then we'll talk.

It's like this. I have no idea how switched on you are about people. I don't know if you notice things or are even aware of anything that goes on every day around you. For example, are you aware of the mannerisms, dress, behaviour and apparent attitudes of the other males and females you encounter every day at work, in the stores, on the street? As a male, probably not, unless it's something truly striking or outlandish. Females on the other hand appear to take in these things naturally. They may or may not retain them for very long, and they may or may not even be aware they are doing it, but they will notice a man's clothes, a woman's hair style, a dress, where a man is looking, what color a woman's shoes are, who is wearing a ring and do it all at a glance.

Domestically, they will, unlike you, be very aware of when the last time was you cleaned up the kitchen, got her something to drink, complimented her, asked how she was feeling (and listened to her reply) or any one of a hundred other little, seemingly insignificant, events. You may or may not hear about it (that depends on your wife's personality and the dynamics of your marriage) but whether you do or do not, if you aspire to perfect husband status, you should start to become very much aware that she is very much aware of what

How to be the Perfect Husband

you do, what you say and how often. In point of fact, yes, she's keeping score.

Then, and perhaps most importantly, is the issue of relationships. As males, we have our own take on relationships. If the relationship is with a female, it usually breaks down into sexual attraction or not. That's a bit simplistic but as a rough description, it'll do. With other males, the relationship is almost always hierarchical. Who is more or less powerful than me? What is my position in the hierarchy and how can I maintain or improve that position? All that said, we don't pay a great deal of attention to male-female relationships in general and are usually unaware of them except in general terms or, at least, of their significance. Besides, who needs all that touchy-feely stuff anyway?

Females, on the other hand, and therefore your new wife, are vastly more aware of relationships. Who is attracted to whom, what different sorts of relationships exist in a group, tensions between individuals, signs and indicators of a relationship's health or lack thereof, etc. One need look no further than 'chick flick' trailers or supermarket magazine covers to see (as the advertizing industry profitably did long ago) the importance females give to relationships. Why this should be so is of only mild interest.[9] What's important is that you be aware that relationships, and all

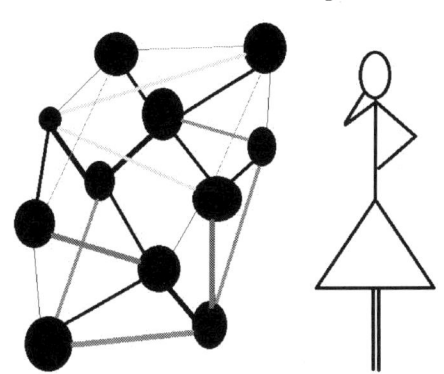

---

[9] There are any number of theories put forward about this but the majority of them seem to center on women being more aware of relationships because, from an evolutionary viewpoint, they have better luck at survival and reproduction if they are. Apparently, through being able to correctly interpret their own relationships with males (potential

that goes on around them, are of considerably greater importance to her than to you.

Taking all that was said in the three preceding paragraphs, it is pretty clear that to understand and respond to your wife as a perfect husband, being merely an ordinary guy with our usual level of attention will simply not cut it. She is operating, at least in many things, at a subtle or nonobvious level and you are going to have to learn, learn to the point where it becomes a habit, to recognize, interpret and respond to those subtleties.

Here's a wee test for you. Answering honestly, how many of the following items about your wife (or potential wife) can you say you know for certain? Do you remember what she was wearing yesterday? Do you remember what you did at home last weekend? Do you recall what the last conversation you had with her was about? Do you know what things make her really angry? Do you know what things she finds mildly annoying? Do you know which of your mannerisms she likes the most? Which ones the least? Do you know what she really thinks of your friends? Do you know what she most wishes would happen and what she most hopes will not? What makes her sad? When was the last time she cried? How many of those items above did you get, or think you got? It is pretty unlikely that she would often come right out and speak with you about any of them. Yet she can answer every one of them

---

mates or dangerous types) and other females (competitors for mates or as aides in the raising of offspring), a female would have an obvious advantage and so, as a gender, they have become pretty good at it. Frankly, I've no idea if any of this is true and for the purposes of becoming a perfect husband, it doesn't really matter. Just be aware that relationships, for whatever reason, are very important to females and therefore to your wife and therefore to you.

How to be the Perfect Husband 17

with dead accuracy because they all matter to her and so, as the perfect husband to be, they must start to matter to you. So how do you do that?

One Word. "Attentive."

And if you forget every other word in the English language, remember that one. Your happy marriage to that woman, your proud title of perfect husband, your degree of future happiness and the enjoyment of what's left of your miserable life may well depend on it.[10] Why?

Before answering why, let's discuss the what. What is this attentive thing?

What attentive is, is actually pretty easy to explain. It quite literally means, paying attention, and in the context of becoming the perfect husband, it means paying attention to her. It means being aware of what she is doing, what she is thinking, of what her opinions are and responding accordingly. Sounds simple, right? Well, it is but don't go confusing simple with easy. Two very different words.

If you have been actually absorbing what you found in the preceding sections of this guide (I'm going to assume that you're nodding yes, here) then you now know at least two things. One, the perfect husband has honestly analyzed himself, knows what and who he is and is comfortable with that. He has nothing to prove or show anyone, including his wife. He is a confident, mature man. He knows himself. And two, women are different. Generally speaking, they are more attuned to, and give greater importance to subtleties

---

[10] But hey, no pressure. Ha!

than most men, particularly the subtleties of relationships.

So, where does and how does this attentive thing fit with those two nuggets? Like this.

Because you are no longer caught up in desperately projecting and defending this image of yourself as a tough, sexy, macho free spirited rebel (as a confident, mature man you can leave all that posing stuff to the little boys), you feel no threat to yourself or your self esteem from considering someone else first. You now have an armoured ego. You are fireproof. You can now focus on what she thinks and what she needs without moaning, as the less than perfect husbands do, "*But what about me?*" As perfect husband material, you are just fine. You don't need reassurance or maintenance.[11] Instead, you are now free to focus on her. And focus on her you must because many of the signs females give regarding their thoughts, feelings and attitudes are subtle ones and not obvious to an average, inattentive male. Being attentive enough to identify and respond appropriately to those things is what separates the perfect husbands from the "also ran's".

Speaking generally, making someone feel good, making someone feel special and important through being attentive to them, is a nice thing to do. As well, it makes you feel good about yourself, but it does more than just that. It also generates a very positive image of you to that person and that's always a good thing. Now imagine that someone is your wife. Clearly, this is a case of not only making someone feel good (someone who you presumably care a great deal about), but it is also very much in your own best interest as well. And as time goes on, it becomes cumulative and generates a permanent cycle. The more attentive to her you are, the more she appreciates you, so you are encouraged to be more attentive to her, so she appre-

---

[11] And if you do still need maintenance, go back and re-read that section about "know yourself" on Page 7 because, clearly, it didn't take the first time.

How to be the Perfect Husband

ciates you more so.........you can see how it goes. Life becomes pretty darned good for everybody.

But....Attentive How?

Everyone knows chivalry is dead, right? All that old-fashioned nonsense about ladies first, holding doors open for women, offering them a seat on a bus, helping her put her coat on, carrying the heavy bags, etc is passé now. Modern women don't want, need or appreciate such sexist, chauvinistic behaviour and detest it when happens. Sure, and the Leafs have a real chance at the Cup this year. This brings us to.....

Courting Behaviour

So, what is human courting behaviour? For a somewhat long and wordy explanation, try Appendix C, but briefly, it is the various efforts, almost universally undertaken by we males, to convince women to marry us. Dates, flowers, gifts, compliments, assurances, displays, etc. The females' role in this dance is mainly one of acceptance or rejection. Some variation by her of a warm "Why yes, I would like to have dinner with you," or a cold glare and "Get lost, creep," pretty much sums it up.

So, what has all this got to do with being the perfect husband? When in pursuit of our intended, we males jump through all the hoops and try everything we can think of to interest and impress the lady. No effort is too great. And if successful, we now have this woman as our wife. So, we don't need to pursue her anymore, right? WRONG. That's an ordinary husband thinking. Perfect husbands, or those who aspire to become one, know that courting behaviour should not end after the marriage ceremony. If you aspire to the degree of happiness and contentment to be found by being a perfect husband, you don't switch off the courting behaviour just because you're now married. Instead, you refine it. You are now cohabiting with the woman you were once only chasing and so, while the tactics shift somewhat, the goal remains the same. To flatter, enchant, impress and sweep her off her feet and convince her that she made an amazingly good choice of males.

But how? What are the rules of this courtship thing that, if followed, can win her heart?

Now you've cracked it! Now you're asking the right questions. This, **this** is the heart of the thing, the perfect husband's 'how to' guide. What follows are 12 solid examples (of the hundreds possible) of attentiveness which the perfect husband will constantly keep in his frontal lobe.

First example. Does your wife like receiving flowers? If she does not, she is a pretty rare female. The vast majority of women LOVE to get flowers. Why? Flowers are just bits of plants, really, that all too soon are going to be brown, dead and mouldy. And we males are pretty blasé about them. So, what's the fascination women have with flowers? Well, they smell and look nice of course, but that's not it. No, it's actually because of what flowers represent. Somebody cared about her enough, and wanted her to know it, to acquire and present them to her. It is a real symbol, one that can be seen, touched and enjoyed (and bragged about) of a relationship she has with an admirer. Remember we talked earlier about the importance of relationships to females? I hope so. Flowers, for women, embody that importance. But perhaps she said to you that she doesn't care whether she gets flowers or not? Yeah, right. And if you'll buy that, I've got some luxury beach front on Hudson's Bay for you. Flowers are always important. Do not forget this.

So, what does this mean to you? You already get her flowers on her birthday and Valentine's Day, right? (*You'd better be nodding yes here, or you are in way worse shape than either of us thought.)* How about this? Flowers every week or whenever the last batch starts to turn brown. Maybe every two weeks. Whatever. The point is, you make sure that on her kitchen counter or office desk or dining room table (the more public the better) there is always a vase of fresh, beautiful flowers. They do not have to be roses (cost too much, die too quick) and they can even have a seasonal theme (winter, spring, Christmas, Halloween, etc) but the key point is that, even if it's just a tiny little bouquet, there is always a fresh, beautiful symbol of your love and affection, right there for her and everyone else to see. In the world of the perfect husband, this one is gold medal stuff. And while we're on the subject, for Valentine's Day, it's **always** red roses. For women, love = red roses.[12] Nothing else cuts it, period. End of discussion. A dozen is the minimum, two dozen is better, but three dozen is too much. You're trying too hard to buy her admiration and it shows.

Tip #3. Want to dress it up a little? When you present her with her regular bouquet, have a small morsel of chocolate, or a miniature of wine or champagne, stashed inside.

Tip #4. Of course, if you are a shmuck, this flower thing could backfire badly. If you continually forget to buy fresh flowers or you put off buying them or promise you'll replace them 'soon', she will have a brown, wilting, sad, visible reminder, reinforced every time she looks at it, of what an uncaring, inattentive loser you really are.

Second Example. Getting her a cup of coffee or tea in the morning is nice. Getting her a cup of coffee or tea, made just the way she likes it, **every** morning, is attentive. Get yourself one too. You've just earned it.

Third Example. Opening a car door for someone is also nice. Depending on the vehicle, these can be awkward things to get in and out of, particularly if a person is encumbered with a briefcase, shopping bag, etc. If it's winter and the footing is not good, it's even more

---

[12] In exactly the same way that the advertizing industry successfully convinced hundreds of millions of women that it was only real, true love if there was a diamond ring attached, they have now also convinced them that only red roses, and nothing else, mean love. Which is perfectly fine as long as you, the guy, understand this going in.

difficult. Or, if they are all dressed up for a date or party, getting in and settled (or out and vertical) can pose some fashion challenges. Opening the car door for your wife (particularly in that date / party example) is not only a public showing to her and the ubiquitous observers of your own gentlemanly qualities as well as your perfect husband attentiveness, it is also just a very nice thing to do for someone. Win, win and win.

Tip #5. As you approach the car, lengthen your stride so as to arrive at her door first. Allow her to slide in at her own speed. Always hesitate for a few seconds to ensure that your lady is comfortably seated, her seat belt is done up and all limbs and clothing are well within the car. Ask if she is comfortable and you may be rewarded with a smile and a nod. Close the door on her coat or foot and you will not.

Fourth Example. There was a time when to take a stroll down a sidewalk was a far less hygienic pastime than today. Passing wagons could spray you with muddy water liberally laced with chunks of horse manure and the contents of chamber pots (i.e.: human waste.). Pedestrians had to be both watchful and quick. Accordingly, back in the day, when a gentleman strolled arm in arm with a lady, he took the side closest to the street so as to protect her from at least some of the filth. That practice, while clearly no longer serving the same purpose, continues today but is rapidly dying out. Too bad. It is a deliciously simple method of racking up points on the perfect husband board without any fear from an assault of flying, and disgusting, waste. When asked why you always move yourself to the street side of a lady (particularly YOUR lady), you gallantly insist that you just don't feel right exposing her to even the theoretical threat of besmirchment. Which may well, in fact, be true.

Tip #6. And just in passing, as we're on the subject of strolling anyway, always initiate the hand-holding or arm-linking. It will be noted by her that it was important to you. More easy points.

Fifth example. There are many rituals associated with your daily life. The morning coffee, the news, breakfast, lunch and supper, getting ready for bed, etc. Women, and so your wife, have many of the same routines. And therein, for the perfect husband, lies opportunity.

We know that women cherish intimacy and we also know they are highly attuned to relationships. Further, we know that they are constantly looking for reassurance that they made the right choice of males. Now suppose you could deliver all that AND enjoy yourself at the same time? Do-able? You bet. Read on.

Every morning you have ensured that she is greeted by a lovely hot cup of tea or coffee (see Second Example). Now if every morning you were to add to it a morning kiss, a brief hug, a question as to how she slept, you have a ritual and one that is not only very pleasing and comforting for her but, really, kind of nice for yourself as well. Imagine that you always (or at least usually) have supper together. Now, I myself use wine (more romantic plus I like wine) but any beverage will do. At the commencement of every supper, before you touch a bite, you (always ensure its you who initiate the action) clink glasses and say, for example, "To us." At the end of every day, as you climb into bed, whether she is awake or asleep (you only THINK you know which), lean over and gently kiss her good night. It is a good idea to do this before turning out the light as it will improve your aim.

All of these rituals, and they are almost infinite in possible numbers, have one critical thing in common. They must be followed every day, without exception. Only occasionally doing so, only every now and then remembering, will just not cut it. It is the ritual nature of the thing that counts. It is the "our special thing" that matters. It is like a shared secret which draws you closer together and she will not only intuitively understand this but will greatly appreciate it also. As will you.

Sixth Example. Today, formal dress is fast disappearing. Except in exceptional circumstance, 'casual dress' has swept the field. Whether this be good or bad, it means that large, heavy, formal coats worn over ladies' elaborate dresses have almost disappeared as has the need for help in putting them on. But the perfect husband is not dismayed. It is the act that counts and holding a light jacket or even a windbreaker at just the right height as to allow her to slip into it gracefully is as much appreciated now as in days of yore. Not to mention that the whole thing has a certain old-world charm. Timing is important. Whether at home or when leaving an establishment, you should arrive at the coat stand or closet slightly ahead and be immediately finding and arranging her coat for her to easily slip into. Fuss a bit to ensure she savours the experience. If she is delayed in the ladies' room, that's a bonus. Take that spare time to get your own coat on. However, if there is no spare time, she always comes first, and you can put your own coat on somehow as you leave. The objects of the exercise (there are several) is to allow her to don her coat with grace, to allow her and any others to see you being the perfect husband and to have her looking and feeling superb as she exits the door. No awkward struggling on the steps. Don't forget her scarf.

And oh, before we hit the Seventh Example, and apropos of public displays of 'perfect husbandness', here's a bit of free advice. Learn to dance. Yeah, you read that right. Learn to dance in that old-fashioned way. Nothing too fancy. Just a basic waltz, a simple foxtrot, that's all it takes. A couple of easy lessons and you're there. There's not a woman in the world who does not and would not be swept off her feet by a man who could take her in his arms and masterfully guide her around a dance floor. It is beyond belief, over the top 'romantic'. It sets you up to look like a worldly, sophisticated, classy guy but that's not the true benefit. The true benefit is your lady's reaction to you publicly (that is, in front of other ladies) showing how well her man treats her and what a fine catch she has made. The fact that you come away looking like some combination of James Bond and Fred Astaire is just the gravy.[13]

Right, back to the examples.

Seventh Example. Opening the door for a woman is, while an admittedly minor exercise, probably the most common of the 'attentive' arts. Most males are at least aware of its existence, even if they do it badly or not at all. Sadly, for both males and females, years of feminist anti-courting propaganda has reduced the frequency with which this pleasant little event happens. But despair not. Here is a vein of pure silver lining which the perfect husband can mine and its roots lie in the point raised very early on in this guide; that of knowing yourself and being confident in all circumstances. Due to that confidence, you are your own man and free to do as you please.

Let the rest of the males be mere nervous cattle, part of that cowed herd. The perfect husband knows that deliberately stepping forward, standing tall and clear-eyed as you hold the door for your lady, is a solid two-pointer. In

---

[13] When the baby boomers convinced their parents back in the 1960s that they should not have to learn how to properly dance in high school, as every previous generation did, those same parents made a huge mistake. By thinking they were doing the caring, liberal thing and caving in to their whining off spring, they condemned them to a life in which those same off spring would never know the pleasure of a couple, together, gently and elegantly gliding across the dance floor. Now, years later, (and unlike previous generations who enjoyed dancing happily and beautifully into very old age) these same offspring, now aged themselves, have only two choices. Try to dance like a teenager and look ridiculous and pathetic or don't dance at all. As has been said, watching your 60 year old father at your wedding trying to dance to Nirvana is just wrong.

fact, your bravely stepping forward in public like that, risking ridicule and disapproval from others so as to do her an old-fashioned courtesy, can give your perfect husband status a very significant leg up. You will note the disapproving scowls on the faces of a few observers (like you care), but it is your wife who will note the many glances of admiration and envy from the vast (mainly female) majority and that will just be the icing on the cake.[14]

Tip #7. A note on technique. Assume you are walking at her side (and holding her hand, of course), as you approach the door. Note which side it opens on. (i.e. where's the handle?) Then, about six feet away, take the one or two extra long strides which will put you at the door just before she reaches it. Then, opening the door with the appropriate hand, gently lay your other hand on her back or shoulder, 'ushering' her through, as it were. Then hurry to catch up and don't forget to pick up her hand again. Simple, really.

Eighth Example. It is 'common knowledge' that girls like shopping and guys don't. Personally, I rarely trust anything considered to be 'common knowledge'. Usually, it's just common nonsense. In the case of shopping though, it seems to actually be true, at least in broad general terms. Most men really don't enjoy the shopping experience, preferring instead to go to a store, select the item they want and leave. This sharply contrasts with many, perhaps most, women's preference for long stretches of extended wandering, looking, checking, comparing. Why this should be so is unknown, at least to me, though I am told it has it's roots in the Palaeolithic age of human development. Maybe so. At any rate, there it is and today it represents an opportunity to be exploited by a clever perfect husband. Go shopping with her. Not all the time, mind you. After a few times doing this, you would not only find shopping with her to be an actively unpleasant experience but, and more importantly from the perfect

---

[14] As an aside, in a misguided effort at being polite, I once held open a door for a woman unknown to me. Not only did she not thank me, she did not even acknowledge my presence, striding through the open door with her nose up, head straight forward and a disdainful expression on her face. I am not normally quick witted but that time, I had the presence of mind to say to her retreating back, (not in a shout, that would have been rude) in a loud, penetrating voice "You're most welcome, I'm sure." Not much of a comeback, it's true, but her step faltered briefly, and the onlookers were amused.

husband perspective, its novelty and impact on your wife would wear off. So, space the number of times you volunteer out a bit. Perhaps once a month or so. Push the cart, carry the packages. Stop for lunch and insist on paying for it, just as if you were on a date. As long as it is only occasional, you can do it with no great difficulty, and she'll love it. A truly perceptive perfect husband might also use the opportunity to observe what kinds of things and colors and styles she seems to prefer. But that would just be gravy. The main point of this exercise is to be seen to sacrifice your happiness and preferences to be with her, as any perfect husband should.

Ninth Example. Housework is women's work, right? Wrong. If this was true in the past, it is not true today and has not been so for a very long time. Probably since our male ancestors had to go out and hunt dangerous critters and battle marauding proto terrorists. Today, there are somewhere between very few and none at all of these manly, brute force jobs left. Our technology has seen to that and so, what excuses for avoiding housework are there left? In fact, none, and the perfect husband not only knows this but has capitalized on it. Rather than dragging his feet and making a big deal out of picking up after himself, today he selflessly volunteers to assist in what customarily was considered, 'woman's work'. Now, there are a number of tactics to keep in mind here. First, make sure you volunteer. If she has to ask for your help, you are already down a notch. You, as an attentive perfect husband, have seen her problem and have stepped forward of your own free will and your concern for her. Next, always select the crappy, dirty jobs, the non-glory ones, the ones she and everybody else do not like but which also have a highly visual, and daily, impact. Dish-washing for instance or taking out the garbage. Neither is particularly difficult, nor particularly time consuming, and so, while they do require a certain discipline on your part to do them every day, they are easily do-able by you.[15] The impression you are trying to make, whether stated out loud or not (your choice here, it's a judgement call), is that from your viewpoint, she is simply too refined and special to be burdened with such low tasks and you are there to take them on in her place.

Tip #8. Look around. There may be other domestic tasks which are also not popular, but which are easily done and high profile and which you could take on, depending on your daily schedule. Dog-walking say, or making the bed every morning, and so consider those as well. And second, never choose any jobs which have cosmetic overtones. Notwithstanding current political correctness, it is still emotionally 'her' house and how it looks is far more critical to her than it is to you. Accordingly, you leave to her such things as setting the table (particularly if there are guests), arranging flowers, dishware, guest rooms, decorations, etc. In fact, anything 'social' is best left to her to arrange as she pleases. Volunteering to wash the outside of the windows though, especially just before a party or an event, is a fine idea.

Tip #9. And a cautionary note: I would here, and again, strongly advise against taking on any task and then failing to see it through. Saying you will wash the dishes or take out the garbage every day and then not doing so is considerably worse than not volunteering in the first place. Before you jump forward, ensure you can carry it through or risk a very real negative mark on your perfect husband score card.

Tenth Example. Closely related to the aforementioned housework, yet still forming a separate category, is volunteering yourself for all the heavy lifting and construction. The shifting of furniture, the moving of boxes and anything involving ladders, power tools or sweat. Why do this? After all, she is, as most females are, quite capable of doing all but the really extreme stuff herself and, depending

---

[15] My Dad taught me the dish washing one, and, I think, his Dad taught him, thus proving that this tactic, amongst the many others, has been played and perfected over generations of perfect husbands.

How to be the Perfect Husband

on the physical abilities of your particular wife, perhaps she can do those extreme things as well. The reasons for volunteering for these types of things are twofold and while the first is an excellent example of attentiveness, the second is an excellent opportunity to reinforce her positive image of you.

First, your offering to do the heavy stuff or construction -related activity implicitly depicts her as delicately feminine. Not helpless, mind you, and it would be wise to point that out at the time. *("Of course, I know you are quite capable of doing it, sweetness, but why strain yourself needlessly? That's what I'm here for.")* But whether she can or can't, you have just given her an opportunity to feel feminine, delicate and special. This is good.

The second is that volunteering gives you the opportunity to show off to your primary audience, this being your wife. You get a chance to show her how strong you are, how clever and skilled you are with tools and raw material, how fit you are and how fine you look in a tight T-shirt. And all in her service and at her beck and call. What a perfect husband you are![16]

Tip #10. A note of caution here. It would be best if you really were strong (or at least stronger than her), you really were fit and that you really do look hot in a tight T-shirt. Also, knowing how to safely operate a power tool might come in handy. Otherwise, the whole thing just might have an

---

[16] There are two sub-sets here which, while not rating their own paragraph, are worth mentioning. These are Reaching/Opening and Killing. Reaching/Opening simply involves reaching all hard to get at shelves, light fixtures, etc. which she finds difficult to reach and, the opening of stubborn bottles or containers. Both give you a chance to help her out, both give you a chance to display your physical prowess, both give her a chance to indulge in a bit of delicate femininity and both are dirt simple. The sub-set labelled Killing is even simpler. It means you kill all creepy crawlies in the house as she discovers them. Fairly straightforward. She is pleased and you look like a fearless hero.

opposite effect to the one intended. Perhaps you should consider having a talk with the hardware store guys and purchasing a gym membership. Soon.

Eleventh Example: Inclusiveness. What's that? In the context of being the perfect husband, it's the tactic of asking her opinion on virtually all subjects. Of enquiring what she thinks of your plan to repair the deck, explaining how you have scheduled your weekend and asking if this works for her, of suggesting you'd like her input about how to cut the grass. Anything at all, including the serious situation developing in the Middle East and what brand of peanut butter is best. It's asking her opinion, even when you have already made up your own mind. But why do this?

There are two reasons to include inclusiveness in your box of perfect husband tools. First, the impression given will be that you value her opinion, that you respect her intellect, her experience and her insight, all of which strokes her ego. Everyone likes to be flattered and this one rebounds nicely onto you. Second, it gives her a distinct feeling of sharing something with you, that you are a team and so, it generates a greater sense of intimacy and of a closer relationship, something most women value greatly. You will look and sound like you actually care which, given that you have chosen to live the rest of your life with her, you had better.

Tip #11. Pay attention when you employ this tactic. It's no good asking her opinion and then turning on the radio, opening a newspaper or falling asleep. Try, through body language and facial expression, to look earnest, engaged and interested. No yawning, sighing or fidgeting.

Tip #12. Assuming my experience is not unique, you will slowly come to realize that she really does have some valuable insight and ideas about various things. You will discover that she, over time, has become a valuable source of information and opinion for you. So here we have a win win. She appreciates you including her, and you gain a useful source of knowledge. Sweet.

Twelfth Example. Compliments. Of all the attentive arts, it is perhaps with compliments that most males find the most difficulty. Some males become so unsure or intimidated by the complexity surrounding compliments that they just don't try any more, feeling silence is safer. While I sympathize with their plight, I also know

How to be the Perfect Husband

that those guys will never attain perfect husband status. While it's true that compliments have the potential to fail and fail badly, they can also, if well considered, win you significant yardage and so, while obviously needing careful handling, compliments should be an integral part of the perfect husband's arsenal.

As you know by now, core issues for males usually center around power; our relative position in the male hierarchy as well as our actual, or perceived, physical strength. For females, it's beauty and her ability to attract and so that's where the perfect husband wants to principally focus his efforts. There are two facets when complimenting females: Subject and timing. First, let's look briefly at timing.

Timing of Compliments. Correctly timing a compliment is directly tied to the perfect husband's level of attentiveness, his degree of focus on his wife's current opinions, attitudes, issues, etc. As a result, the perfect husband knows when his wife is happy or unhappy with something and that dictates when or when not, to compliment. For example, your wife has just returned from the hairdresser. Is it time to compliment or not? Maybe yes, maybe no. Let's dissect the moment and then decide.

First off, you must be aware that she actually went to her hairdresser which, as the perfect husband, you, of course, are. Second, you should be aware, at least in a general sense, of her hair issues.

Does she dye her hair, does the style change a lot and so forth. I know, for guys, this is hard. We don't really know or even particularly care about hair stuff beyond a general, does it look nice? Not so women. Hair is a large issue for them and so, should not be commented on lightly. Returning to our example, she's back and appears pleased, her body language is good, and her hair looks nice (not that you can really tell but anyway....) so a compliment is therefore appropriate.[17] But what to say? Short and positive is always the best way to go. You noticed her 'new' hair which is worth a couple of points and you think it makes her look great, which is a couple more. "Wow, your hair looks really great" about sums it up. Do not go into details, which you don't grasp anyway, and do not offer your opinion on why it is 'better' than before. That way lies quicksand. Short and positive wins the day. Collect your points and walk away. Over the next day or so, a couple of additional, "Your hair looks really good." can be lobbed but don't extend it beyond that. Your compliment will begin to lose its strength if overused. However, and unrelated to any actual hairdresser visits, an occasional, "Your hair looks nice," given always just after you (cleverly) noted she's brushed or washed it, will be well received.

Bravo!

Any questions on the timing of compliments? To put it in a nutshell, time your compliment to closely follow your wife's events (of which as a perfect husband, you keep yourself well apprised) such as hair appointments, new clothes she just bought, a lovely meal she recently made, her preparation for a party and so forth. She has just made an effort at something. Now is the time for you to step forward and say the right thing about that effort. Later will look and sound pretty lame.

Subject of Compliments. After the 'Timing' of compliments, there is the 'Subject'. What to compliment is always a major issue for guys. Do I say something nice about her eyes? Do I favourably

---

[17] Conversely, if she comes back in tears or furious and says something like "Look what they did to my hair!" it's a fair bet a compliment is a bad idea. Sympathetic noises and a willingness to listen are all you should venture at a time like that. She is upset about something important to her and if you start giving your uninformed and useless opinion, you could easily attract her anger onto yourself.

How to be the Perfect Husband

comment on her choice of clothes? Do I put forward how successfully she seems to be losing weight? Clearly, it's a minefield and unless you think you might enjoy getting a leg blown off, you want to tread very carefully here.

Weight. First, let's talk about weight or more accurately, let's not. ANY discussion of ANYTHING related to female weight is off limits. Yes, there are tricks and techniques, but they reside in the realm of the "advanced perfect husband" and are not for the likes of you. Just don't go there. If she raises the subject, you ignore it and/or run the other way. Fake a heart attack, fake Alzheimer's, whatever. You cannot win by trying to address this subject. All you can do is lose and, at least potentially, lose badly. So, remember, no compliments about weight, period. "You look great!" begins and ends it.

Age. Female age runs a close second to weight in terms of sensi-

tivity. While not as potentially lethal as weight, it is a subject which should generally not be raised by the perfect husband. You know how old she is, she knows that you know, so there is little for a perfect husband to gain, and considerable potential to lose, from raising the subject with her or allowing a conversation to go in that direction. Having said that, always remember her birthday. Just be sure to conveniently forget which birthday it is.

Hair. I think hair was adequately covered previously. Just be aware it's a very big deal for women and proceed accordingly. Noticing is very good. Attempting to comment on it knowledgably is almost always very bad.

Eyes / Makeup. A beautifully made-up female face and eyes are a lovely thing to behold and are very much worthy of complimenting. She has made an effort, probably for you, and so she has earned and deserves praise. The only cautionary note here is that, like hair, it is unlikely you understand exactly what is involved and so, keep your sincere compliments general in nature.

Dress. You have absolutely no knowledge regarding female fashion and we both know it. Giving your honest opinion will either confuse her or hurt her feelings or both. Why do that? Listen carefully to her as she shows off her new article or outfit to you. What that object is has no relevance. What really counts is how pleased she is or is not with it. As a general rule, she would not be showing it to you if she did not think it was, at least in general terms, a good thing and so, that's the route you take. Always appear interested and try to match her level of enthusiasm for the object. Parrot back to her some of the words she uses. It looks 'good', or 'classy' or 'sophisticated' but let it go at that. Leave it to her female friends and relatives to sort out what may or may not be a fashion disaster.

Cooking. Now here you have a good shot at real compliments. If she is a good cook, you should tell her so. Within limits, say what you think. She has either a natural talent or has worked hard at it and in either case, you are the beneficiary. Say so in front of others too. If she is a not so good cook, she does not need your criticism. She needs encouragement and, unless you want to both hurt her feelings and have crap dinners for the rest of your life, it's up to you to deliver. Try to eat what's put in front of you and with no gagging. The words used here are very important. It's never *'awful'*, it's *'close but needs a bit of something'*. It's never *'another failure'*. It's *'a clear improvement and very promising'*. A budding cook can be crushed by a few ill-chosen words and in the long run, the real loser will be you.

Tip #13 .I have found it useful to loudly mention that washing up all the dishes, pots and pans after dinner (which I unfailingly do) is a small and completely reasonable price to pay for having someone prepare yet another exquisite meal which, by the way and over time, they now all are.

House. Anything she has just finished to her satisfaction (curtains, decorating, cleaning, whatever) should be praised. She is already pleased with her own efforts and your giving her a compliment at just that moment will simply increase a level of happy which is already there. An easy score for a perfect husband.

Attentiveness Summarized.

And so, to summarize attentiveness, the following. While all those things mentioned above (holding open doors, especially car doors, helping with her coat, etc) are good and worth doing, three general things regarding attentiveness should be kept in mind:

First, be consistent. If you are going to do it, do it all the time. Sometimes holding a door (or a coat or whatever) and sometimes not sends a confusing signal. If you were doing it and then forget or don't bother, she may think you are mad about something or are losing interest in her and that can just turn into a mess. Become reliable.

Second, don't make too big a show about it. A casual yet dignified attentiveness is much classier than leaping around like a puppy or shouting, both of which would almost certainly only make you look stupid and embarrass her. Dignified attentiveness. Rest assured, she will notice.

The third and final thing is that all these things (doors, coats, and heavy packages, whatever) are usually public or semi-public displays of affection and deference. Lots of other women are watching closely even if you, mere male that you are, don't catch them doing so. Your wife knows this too. The paying of a public compliment, which is what you are doing, has a direct and immediate impact on her ego and so, has a direct and immediate impact on how she feels about herself and about you. These nice, attentive actions of yours are usually small and seemingly minor but they can and will have a very large influence on your overall perfect husband status. Though they seem minor or trivial, do not overlook or dismiss their importance because, rest assured, she won't.

Sex

For something that occupies so much of our time, energy, and thoughts, there is surprisingly little to say about sex from the perfect husband perspective. Be kind, be patient and remember that having sex is not, for women, the basic, stand-alone, mechanical act it is for men. For women, it's a part (obviously a very important part) of a bigger relationship. There's that word again.

It is here, probably as much or more than anywhere else in the world of the perfect husband, that the truth about 'knowing yourself', discussed earlier, holds true. If you really are the self confident, mature male you by now should be, you have no need to control or dominate the sexual relationship you have with your wife. You can afford to be the kind, patient, thoughtful lover. It costs you nothing and will reap huge benefits' in terms of how she thinks about you both in the bedroom and more generally. Have fun.

Cheating on your Wife

Don't. Just don't. Males are inclined that way, it's true. While you might want to refer back to Appendix A for the reasons, the bottom line is that it would take a fairly unusual male who, if between the ages of about 15 and 80, would not have his head turned by the display of a nicely curved hip or a wee bit of cleavage. In fact, we are programmed by evolution to do exactly that. This does not, however, translate into 'it's okay for guys because we need sex more'. Males do indeed want large amounts of sexual activity, particularly when young, but so what? Think that's an excuse? If you figure having only one female bedmate is just not enough, don't get married in the first place. If you are already married and your wife is not providing, and you believe will never provide, what you feel you need, get safely divorced. But if your plan is to marry her, keep her sleeping only with you, while at the same time you get to bonk everything in a skirt, good luck and see you in court.

How to be the Perfect Husband

Can you get away with cheating? Assuming you are of average intelligence, probably for a while, but there are some very serious caveats attached which you would be wise to consider.

First, you won't get away with it forever. Sooner or later, you will make a mistake or your wife (or her friends) will twig to something. Or you may just encounter bad luck. Regardless, sooner or later, odds are you will be found out and confronted. Are you prepared to explain your actions to your wife and others?

Second, smart as you think you are, you ain't that smart. If you cheat on your wife, and unless you are a professional spook, you are going to leave a trail. Dates, times, logbooks, credit card bills, ATMs, purchases, CCTV, phone records, enemies, a slip of the tongue, Internet accounts, random sightings, investigators, etc. If the whole thing turns ugly, and eventually it is almost bound to, you will have left a trail of ammunition which her lawyer is going to gleefully fire straight at you in court. What could have been a sad but relatively straightforward case of divorce based on incompatibility could now, spurred on by her anger at your lies and treachery, very easily become a full-blown, life-altering, train wreck for you. If her lawyer is even halfway competent, they will be holding all the evidence of your guilt up in front of a judge and you can expect to be, financially speaking, gutted like a fish and in public too. You up for that, buddy?[18]

Finally, there is this. Every day, you get out of bed and look in the mirror. If you cheat on your wife, that guy looking back at you is, and is now known by others to be, a cheat, a liar, an oath-breaker, someone who gave his word and then broke it, who betrayed a trust,

---

[18] And if you have screwed around on her after any kids have arrived, it gets far, far worse. You will have an open wound in your wallet that will drain your income for decades. We are talking hundreds and possibly thousands a month. Yes, a month.

who went back on his solemn promise. You are not a cool player, you are not virile manly guy, you are not a smart operator. You are a sneaking, dishonourable little shit who nobody, including you, will ever really like or trust again. Congratulations. While you will have failed big time at becoming a perfect husband, you will have swept to success as the perfect fool.[19]

Telling the Truth

Most of us were brought up to always tell the truth, or at least to know that telling the truth was 'good' and not telling it was 'bad'. Still, in the course of a normal life, all of us develop our own standards when it comes to telling the truth. Some do so all the time, some most of the time, some do so when it suits their purposes, and some tell the truth only when a lie won't work.

Some time ago (in fact, quite a few years ago now) I discovered something I am going to share with you, no charge. Consider it just part of what you paid for with this guide. For anyone, and for the perfect husband in particular, always telling the truth is a really, really smart thing to do. Why?

It might be because telling the truth gains you the moral high ground or because it's the 'right' thing to do, both of which, of course, are quite true. But the main reason, like the whole concept of being a perfect husband and as stated right at the beginning of this guide, is because:

"It is in your own best interest!"

Think of it this way. There's the truth. It's uncomfortable

---

[19] As an aside, I have met and worked with many men who I liked, admired and trusted. Others, I did not. While I cannot say that all those I did not like were cheaters, I can say this. All the cheaters who I came to know about I did not like or trust. If they'll lie to their wife, they'll lie to you.

and / or embarrassing so instead of being up front and telling it to your wife, you tell a lie in an attempt to hide it. That is a mistake. Maybe you told the lie to cover up something you just forgot to do, maybe because you decided something else was more important or, maybe because you know damn well you are in the wrong and are trying to hide it. But by lying, you are about to make it all worse.

Telling that lie now means you must always remember that you told it and so avoid anything which may reveal that you lied. Second, it will almost certainly lead to a supplementary lie, needed to cover up the first one. Now you have two (or more). And third, you have set yourself a pattern of lying. You now begin to do so automatically, the cover stories multiply, and the complexity and danger increase. Trust between you and your wife decreases, suspicions grow. Life becomes less happy. And if she catches you out, it becomes very much less happy.

Telling the truth is enormously liberating. There is an incredible sense of freedom when you are telling the truth. You don't have to remember a cover story, you don't have to dovetail your lie with anything else, you don't have to check the angles, arrange an alibi or remember what you said previously. You just have to tell the truth. Sometimes this may be awkward, even uncomfortable or briefly embarrassing but, and I guarantee this, in the long run it is really, really worth it.

Might she occasionally be pissed off with your telling her the truth? Yeah, maybe. And so, if the question is something like "Do you think I'm fat?" then lie your fool head off. But if it is something else, something actually important such as where you have been or what were you doing or where's the money, then the straight up truth is the way to go, every time. Uncomfortable at the time maybe, but in the long run, you feel way better, you feel way freer, you feel way more positive about yourself AND you gain a reputation with your wife and others for always speaking the truth. Priceless. One final gift from telling the truth: the whole issue of honesty for you becomes just one less thing to think and worry about in your complex, complicated and confusing world. Telling the truth is the way to go.

The Perfect Husband, summarized

Well then, that's it. If you have read and absorbed all that is written above, you are now in possession of the tools which, properly used, can assist you in becoming a perfect husband. To summarize:

First and foremost, **know yourself**. If you are still trying to be one of the lads, partying, playing the field and deeply concerned about what the other guys think about you, then it's time to change. Otherwise, forget the perfect husband thing. You are not ready for it and may never be. Perfect husband status is reserved for those who are mature enough to see themselves for what they really are and who have the confidence that comes with this knowledge. Without that self confidence, that belief in yourself, you will never be able to put someone else, your wife, first.

Next (with a nod to Footnote 4), **choose the optimum woman**. If you are choosing based on beauty or bra size or wealth, you are missing the boat. If you are choosing based on what you have in common, on what kind of a person she is and her own level of maturity and confidence, you have a real chance. Marriage is a big deal. You are going to live with this person every day from now on. Think past the immediate and try to imagine you both in your 40s or 50s. If you are in doubt, don't do it.

Then, **become attentive**. Women are different. While every bit as smart and capable as us, they think differently than we males. Understand and accept this. Only through paying close attention to what your now wife does, thinks and says will you be able to respond beyond her expectations. If this seems too hard or you are too selfish or too lazy, then marriage is probably not for you and the status of perfect husband will probably never be yours.

And finally, and with admitted exceptions, you know that women in general (and yours in particular), are wonderful creatures. You knew this before you married her and, so, you pulled out all the stops (dates, compliments, flowers, attentiveness, etc.) to prove to her that you were the man of her dreams and to win her heart. Now that you have succeeded, don't stop. Unless you want the marriage ceremony itself to be the high point, and everything after that to be downhill, don't stop. Keep the courtship going. Prove to her every day, in a hundred small ways, that you are as pleased and grateful now for her choosing you as you were way back when she said yes. The pay-back from this, the waking up every morning with a partner who you love and trust and who loves and trusts you, is literally priceless. And the title of Perfect Husband, well and truly earned, will be well and truly yours.

Good luck and all the best.
Mungo Auchinleck

The Appendices

Frankly, it's almost embarrassing how dumb my own gender can be sometimes. Initially, I gave no thought at all to adding any explanatory Appendices to this guide. Why would I? It was only after numerous discussions with other males that the realization dawned on me that many of them had amazingly little idea (and even less understanding) of basic human processes and behaviour, including their own.[20] That's when I decided a simply worded glossary, in the form of Appendices, might be useful to my sometimes woefully ignorant brothers.

And so, pedantic, simplistic and long-winded as they unquestionably are, here are three basic things.

Appendix A: Reproductive Strategies

Why is becoming enamoured about a sexually attractive female the most common male weakness? Okay, time for a replay of your high school biology class. The starting premise for all this is that male and female fashions change, attitudes change, opinions change, gender roles change but that all of that is just the shallow upper level, only inches deep and only in the last ten thousand years or so. What males and females really are and how they really interact evolved over millions of years and is miles deep. It is embedded in our DNA and, regardless of past, current or future 'changes', will continue to shape what we pretend today are our 'free choices' regarding the actions of both males and females.

As you know (or perhaps vaguely remember?), the end game of all life on our planet is survival and successful reproduction (in a real sense, the same thing.) and it pretty much drives how all life acts. All species, all life forms, no exceptions. Focusing just on our species (though it holds true for most of the others as well) the male

---

[20] While researching this guide, I heard a very young man wondering (or perhaps he was complaining) that if women were really equal like everybody said, then how come, with condoms and the pill readily available, they were not as eager to jump into bed as he was? Clearly, yet another sad case of someone confusing equality with sameness. Probably never heard of evolution either.

reproduces through having sex, the female from giving birth. The end goal is identical (successfully passing on your DNA) but *the two reproductive strategies could not be more different*. Males are working for quantity. Find a female, convince her to mate with you, move on and find another female. Repeat until you die. Theoretically, he could successfully reproduce every day. In a perfect male world, not only is he free to chase any female at any time but he will be her first and last partner and she will only ever bear his offspring. Yeah, right, and clearly unworkable, particularly in modern, complex human societies, but at least it explains our fixation on sex. When women complain that *"Men only want one thing!"* they have a sadly valid point. Buts that's evolution for you.

Females, on the other hand, with a vastly greater reproductive investment (they get pregnant, we don't) are going not for quantity but for quality. With a ceiling of, roughly, only one (or less) successful reproductions per year, she has to get it right. IE: the best available male (what this means will vary widely) amongst those available in her place and time. Sex is obviously a critical part but, unlike us males, it's only a part. They have to also consider genetics, successfully getting pregnant, surviving giving birth, her biological clock, raising the outcome for the next 15 years, etc, etc. Part of that etc is: can the potential father be relied on to be around to protect and provide while the female and any offspring are vulnerable? A female's chances of successfully reproducing go way, way up if she has a high quality (relatively speaking) male around to provide and protect. Because marriage (or an equivalent) more or less ensures this, no surprise that the wedding day is referred to not as his but 'her big day'. She has taken a giant step forward in the direction of successful reproduction. This is a.k.a. commitment. Given the males relentless efforts to lure them into bed and the potential costs to females of allowing this to happen, its little wonder they have been programmed to be sceptical when it comes to male promises and assurances. You may have noticed this.[21]

---

[21] Some advice here. It's a really good idea to keep any understanding of the subconscious working of the female mind to yourself. She very, very much wants to believe that the entire marriage thing is first, last and only about love, devotion and finding a 'soul mate' and that the babies are just a kind of happy, blissful afterthought which somehow follow from your mutual adoration. Happy announcements such as "WE are pregnant." should be swallowed by you without comment. The fact that you know otherwise is not only not particularly important but will only sadden and disappoint her if you are stupid enough to bring it up. So, why not shut the heck up and go along?

The entire above process, for both males and females, is millions of years old and utterly instinctive, and so, no conscious thought required on your part, which is, given the intellectual level of the average male, a good thing. (Admit it. You slept through Evolutionary Biology.) Now, if you don't really want to think about all this, that's fine. But if you really don't know that it's out there in the background and operating, you're dumber than you look. That noise you hear is the sound of her subconscious evaluating your reliability and commitment potential.

For the perfect husband, the takeaway here is that you must, (note I didn't say may) must be aware that she has interests and concerns that are not, as ours's are, focused primarily on sex. She is also, and simultaneously, reacting to concerns about relationships, reliability, sincerity, commitment, etc. Sexual relations are just one of a number of issues for her and the perfect husband understands this and responds accordingly.

Appendix B: The Selection Process

Rather than clutter up the text of this guide with an explanation about the selection process, I'll drop it in here where it can be ignored more easily. As you were perhaps shown somewhere in Biology, Anthropology or Sociology 101, the selection process in our species is basically a three-part process, the first two parts being carried out by only the female and the third by both genders simultaneously. The first part consists of the female making herself as attractive as possible, the object being to attract the largest pool of males possible so her choices will be broader. Given the fixation of most males on simple lust, and our general interest in any female who can fog a mirror, this should not be difficult but remember, she is looking for the best available male, not just anybody with a Y chromosome. (Yes, a Y chromosome means it's a guy. Good guess.)

The second part consists of her evaluation of this group of lusting males in terms of general health and genetic potential. Most of this is automatic and instinctive. The male's age (that one is a critical factor), size, musculature and features (hair, teeth, facial features, etc) are noted immediately and automatically. Simultaneously, she checks his demeanor. Specifically, does he appear (based largely on how he moves and interacts with other males) powerful, confident and well placed in the male hierarchy? All of this will give her an idea if this guy is even in the running.

Assuming the answer is yes, the third part of the evaluation kicks in. This takes considerably longer because it requires the male, now actively involved, to convince her that he is great with children, that he is, or will be, loyal to her alone and also that he can and will support her and her offspring when they appear. Her evaluation of this third part will decide the issue.

Clearly it is then in our best interests (us being the males) to become pretty good at advertising ourselves in general through appearance and action *(I'm young, strong, and powerful with great genes!)*. And having made the cuts and entered the third part (see previous paragraph), we have to be pretty good at convincing the female that this particular male is the one *(I'm utterly hooked on you to the exclusion of all others forever. Oh, and I like kids!)*. Also, clearly then, it is in her best interest to become very good at observation and evaluation with a strong bias towards scepticism. (As an aside, I have always suspected that the well-known yet unproven "female intuition" may be nothing more than a spinoff of this need for skilled, critical observation and analysis, but I digress.) After many millions of years of work, evolution has ensured that both genders adopt these roles automatically. Any apparent variations to it (and these are almost limitless) are culturally based and do not affect the underlying instinct.

And the takeaway for a perfect husband? As much as possible, keep yourself looking like a real catch. Keep in at least fair physical shape. Keep the courtship going. Even long after she has accepted you as her lifetime partner, continue to treat her as if she was still your goal to be attained.

Appendix C: Courting Behaviour

So just what the heck is this courting behaviour thing? And why should I care? The purpose of human courting behaviour, almost universally conducted by a male, is to convince a female to mate with / marry him. In fact, you yourself have done this, probably numerous times. "Hey baby, buy you a drink?" is the low end of the scale here. Thankfully, it gets better and at the upper end are quite sincere, earnest and honest declarations of love, fidelity and commitment. In between lies every imaginable ploy, tactic and strategy that we males can conceive of to lower the guard of the female. And as always, it is left to the female to sort out the sheep from the goats.

In our culture, courting behaviour (sometimes called "wooing") has generally come to mean the actions of a male trying to convince a female to marry him. These consist of a combination of efforts, some to show what good mate material (*look how big, strong, handsome, rich, powerful, confident and child-friendly I am*) he would be and others to show how much he cares for and respects her. So why do we do this?

Now, this pisses off the feminists (that's just a bonus) but in our species, like most others, males instinctively want to court females. It's not a cultural thing or learned behaviour, it's biological. It's in our DNA, put there over millions of years of evolutionary development for the very best of evolutionary reasons: Successfully courting females, that is convincing her that we are a good catch both in terms of genetics and in the protector / provider roles, vastly improves our chances of successful reproduction. By the same token, and for the exact same reason, females want to be courted. (See Appendix B: The Selection Process) The actual characteristics of that courtship, male or female, will vary enormously based on region, culture, religion, circumstances and period of history you're in but take place they will and no amount of propaganda or legislation can ever stop them. In our own time and culture, courtship behaviour has been changing radically and will continue to do so but that fundamental desire to court and be courted remains unchanged. Mother Nature insists.

So, what's the takeaway here for the perfect husband? You instinctively knew, and acted on the knowledge, that females instinctively need and want to be courted. And it worked. Good for you. Now, don't stop doing this just because you succeeded in getting her to marry you. Every day, continue the courtship.

Notes

Printed in Great Britain
by Amazon